BEFORE I GO

PREPARING YOUR AFFAIRS
FOR YOUR HEIRS

ARIE J. KORVING

KORVING AND COMPANY, LLC
SUFFOLK, VIRGINIA

Korving & Company LLC
Financial Planning & Asset Management
1510 Breezeport Way, Suite 800
Suffolk, Virginia 23435
www.korvingco.com

ISBN 978-0-9838785-0-6

Cover and text design by John Reinhardt Book Design

Printed in the United States of America

CONTENTS

Introduction

A man should not leave this earth with unfinished business.
He should live each day as if it was a pre-flight check.
He should ask each morning, am I prepared to lift-off?

Diane Frolov and Andrew Schneider
Northern Exposure, All is Vanity, 1991

As a CERTIFIED FINANCIAL PLANNER™ professional, I have worked with hundreds of individuals and families, helping them plan for important events in their lives. For younger families, those events may include buying a home and saving for college. As families age, planning for retirement takes center stage. Older couples focus on making sure that their spouses are taken care of and considering what assets and instructions they want to leave for the next generation. Although people mean well, their plans usually go no further than preparing wills and trusts.

One thing is nearly universal. No matter how well the estate plan is drawn, the spouse or other survivors left behind frequently have a difficult time coping, and not always for the obvious reason. Of course, emotions of grief and loss after the death of a loved one infuse all activities. When a spouse or parent dies, however, the survivors are required to make a series of difficult decisions immediately after death, when they are least able to focus clearly. That's because most plans are drawn with an eye to the big picture.

1

Unfortunately, as the old saying goes, "the devil is in the details." We live in a world where questions demand immediate answers from your survivors. What kind of funeral? What burial type and place shall we choose? What about life insurance, and how do your beneficiaries contact the insurance company? Who else needs to be contacted? If bills are paid via automatic withdrawals or electronic bill payment, what is the user name and password for bill paying and other electronic accounts? What will the surviving spouse's income be? How will he or she manage financially? Who should the heirs rely on for trusted advice?

A few years ago I realized that when I die, my wife would have a difficult time taking control of those aspects of our lives that I have always managed during our marriage. She's a very capable woman, but I decided to create a guide to make things easier for her if I die first. I created an "instruction manual" for her.

Now, I've decided to share it with you, so that you too can help your loved ones. A little work and planning now will make it much easier for those you leave behind. By completing the accompanying workbook you will enable your loved ones to focus on exactly what they need to do—mourning your death and remembering you fondly.

The purpose of this manual is to help you do the following:

- Record your wishes in the event you become terminally ill or incapacitated.
- List the information survivors will need for your death certificate and other documents.
- Recount how and where you want to be buried.
- List your regular household expenses, and how to pay any recurring bills or stop any automatic withdrawals.
- Provide an estimate of what the survivor's income may be upon your death.
- Give guidance about the location of your investments and how they should be managed.
- Describe how to collect on your life insurance.
- Explain other benefit programs to which your loved ones may be entitled.

- Provide an easily accessible place for any other personal issues or instructions that you may have.

Even if you are young and healthy this book can help you. When I described this book to a thirty-something nurse, she said: "Great! You know, if my husband should die, I don't even know what insurance policies he has or what his 401k is worth. Hurry up and write it."

No matter your age, my hope is that this instruction manual and the accompanying workbook will help you help your loved ones when you are gone.

CHAPTER ONE

MESSAGE TO THE FAMILY

*Death is a comingling of eternity with time; in the death of a
good man, eternity is seen looking through time.*

JOHANN WOLFGANG VON GOETHE

T he old saying about death and taxes being the only things that
are certain in life is only partly true. Taxes change. Death is
certain. The end of our lives is something that we face only
reluctantly, if at all. When someone close to us dies, the effect is always sadness. When a spouse or parent dies, the effect is traumatic.

Because death is an unpleasant subject, most of us simply refuse to
think about it and what it means to those around us. Unfortunately,
the refusal to think about death often multiplies the stress on those
who are left behind.

Sue Smith (not her real name) became a widow after her husband,
Sam's, brief illness. Sam had been an executive at a large corporation
for many years and had retired. He had been a take-charge guy all
his life, both at work and at home. He had been the primary income
earner, made the investment decisions, paid the bills, and did everything he could do to make Sue happy. And they were, until Sam's
unexpected death. Suddenly Sue was alone.

In a matter of hours Sue had to make a large number of decisions.
Some required immediate action, such as the selection of a funeral

home and the arrangement of the church service and internment. Some decisions she was forced to face over the following weeks: What was her income? Did she have any debts? What bills needed to be paid now and what could be paid later? What were her financial assets? What about estate taxes, insurance policies, and annuities?

Sue was overwhelmed. This was a crushing burden to fall on someone who had never been required to take care of these things. She felt like a child, dropped in the middle of dark woods with wild animals prowling around. The result was not only deep sadness but also paranoia. Since her husband had always taken care of the family finances, she felt unprepared to handle major decisions and was terrified of being victimized. And because Sam had not left an instruction manual for her, Sue went through a long period of grief combined with anger, confusion, and fear. Sad to say, Sue never overcame the issues that surfaced after her husband's death, and it made her life as a suddenly single person very unhappy.

Perhaps you don't have a spouse or a life partner. No matter. All of us need someone to take care of our affairs when we die. This guide will help you to help that person, whoever they may be. One lasting act of kindness you can give your children or surviving relatives and friends is to follow this guide and complete the workbook detailing your final instructions. Having all the most important details in one place will reduce the stress and strain on your loved ones.

Death, even a death that is anticipated, often leaves many unresolved questions about how to proceed. By completing the workbook, your family will know all that they need to know regarding your wishes, from the beginning of your final illness, and it will make it a little easier for them to adjust to the new normal of life without you.

Before we get into more practical details, let me admit something. I did not grow up in a very touchy-feely family. We did not often show or talk about our emotions. I regret that, before they died, I did not have the courage to tell my parents how much they meant to me. I always felt it was never the right time or there was never the opportunity. But before he died, my father wrote me a letter, in his broken English, that I will always treasure because it said—with humor and warmth—how much he loved my family and me.

If talking face to face with your family about your feelings is difficult—as it is for many people—then write a message or letter to them. They will treasure it all the days of their lives. You might write one letter or message to everyone. Or you could write individual letters to particular loved ones.

If you wish, you may use the workbook that was designed as a companion for this guide. You may record your final message there. Look for the box below the heading, "To my family and friends, this is my gift to you."

CHAPTER TWO

FINAL ILLNESS—OR IS IT?

Death is the best part of life. That's why they save it for last.

SOLOMON SHORT

When we are young, we feel immortal. As we age, life's wear and tear brings health care to our minds. Get two or more retirees together and the discussion will invariably come around to the latest aches and pains. The older we get, the more we tend to wonder if an illness will be our last one.

When he was 73, my brother-in-law almost died. While at home, he collapsed with a aortic aneurysm. Paramedics were called and he was taken to the hospital. Half of the patients with this kind of a rupture don't survive the trip to the hospital. He arrived in a coma. For a person of his age, this kind of medical catastrophe is almost always fatal. The doctors suggested to my sister that it was best to let him go peacefully. Even if they were to stabilize him, the chances of his recovering were almost nil. My sister wouldn't hear of it and demanded that they do everything to save her husband. He lingered in a coma for four weeks. His family took turns sitting at his bedside. Suddenly, one day, he woke up. He lived normally for more than a decade longer, giving his family much happiness.

The issue of how "heroic" life sustaining efforts should be is deeply personal. The subject should be discussed with family members before the need arises. Most of us have seen friends or relatives sustained only by a glittering array of machines that perform the functions of failing hearts, lungs, and other vital organs. The ability of modern medicine to prolong life is amazing. Each of us has to decide to what extent we wish to have our lives sustained under these circumstances.

As an independent man or woman, you want to receive the best medical treatment. But you also want control of your medical treatment. That is why doctors explain the various benefits and risks of medical procedures that we may be asked to undergo.

You are entitled by law to make medical choices, even if you are too ill to make your wishes known. If you are conscious, your physician will explain the options for you. What happens, however, if you are unable to speak for yourself?

You can decide in advance what types of treatment you are willing to accept if you are terminally ill or have an injury with no reasonable chance of recovery. You can record your wishes, in advance, in a document called an Advance Directive. And you can record your decisions in the U.S. Living Will Registry.

ADVANCE DIRECTIVE

An Advance Directive is a witnessed, written legal document that clearly states your choices of medical treatment. You must sign it in the presence of two witnesses who also sign it. Witnesses cannot be blood relatives or a spouse.

Virginia, the state in which I reside, recognizes three types of Advance Directives:

- A *Living Will*
- An appointment of a *Healthcare Agent*
- Choices about making a *gift of your body organs*

Your state may have different regulations regarding this issue, so this is an area you should discuss with your family as well as a competent attorney familiar with your state law.

A Living Will sets forth your intentions with respect to medical decisions in the event you become incapacitated and are unable to make such decisions on your own behalf. For example, a Living Will may provide your instructions for use of dialysis or breathing machines, resuscitation if breathing or heartbeat stops, use of feeding tubes, and organ or tissue donation upon death. A Living Will should be created in conjunction with a Durable Power of Attorney for Healthcare.

A Durable Power of Attorney for Healthcare [DPA] allows you to appoint someone to act and make healthcare decisions on your behalf. The "durable" aspect refers to the fact that the agent you appoint can act if you become incapacitated. These documents are not always accepted by all institutions, so check with those organizations with whom your DPA will most likely need to interact.

A Durable Power of Attorney for Healthcare may also be called a "healthcare agent," "healthcare proxy," or a "healthcare declaration." The person you choose as your agent should be someone you trust. The person should understand what you value, how you view end-of-life issues, and what you most likely would choose if you were able. You should discuss all of these issues with the person you choose.

An example of an Advance Medical Directive is located in the workbook.

IMPORTANT NOTE: You should consult an attorney regarding specific laws for these documents in your state.

You may also want to check with a local hospital or your physician for more information. Alternatively, you can find information online about Advance Directives or Living Wills. The following organizations and websites contain helpful information as well as forms you can print and use: National Hospice and Palliative Care Organization at www.nhpco.org, National Institutes of Health's MedlinePlus, AARP, FamilyDoctor.org, Mayo Foundation for Medical Education and Research, American Hospital Association, and AGS Foundation for Health in Aging.

The subject of Advance Directives is complex and involves terms with which you may not be familiar. The following are some common legal terms that you will find in wills, trusts and other legal documents and their definitions.

Administrator—A person appointed by the court to manage your estate when you die without leaving a will. Since they are court appointed, they are required to post a bond as security. They have similar duties as an executor.

Attorney-in-Fact—The individual who is designated in the power of attorney document to act as agent for another.

Beneficiary—Someone entitled to a benefit under a will, trust, or contract, such as an insurance policy.

Crummey Powers—A power in a trust that allows trust beneficiaries to withdraw all or a portion of a contribution to the trust for a limited period of time. Allows the contribution to qualify for the annual gift tax exclusion.

Domicile—The permanent residence of a person or the place to which the person intends to return even though he or she may actually reside elsewhere.

Durable Power of Attorney—A written legal document that lets an individual designate another person to act on his or her behalf, even in the event the individual becomes disabled or incapacitated.

Durable Power of Attorney for Healthcare—A written legal document that gives another person the power to act on your behalf with regard to your healthcare decisions.

Estate—The property or assets you own or have rights to.

Estate Tax—The tax imposed at a person's death on the transfer of most types of property.

Executor—A person named in your will to manage your estate. This person will collect your property, pay any debts and taxes, and distribute your property or assets according to your will.

Fiduciary—A person or institution who is legally responsible for the management, investment, and distribution of funds for another and who must exercise a standard of care imposed by law or contract (e.g., a trustee, executor, administrator, conservator, guardian, or certain investment managers).

Grantor—The person who transfers assets to a trustee to be held for the benefit of another.

Guardian—The person legally entrusted with the care of a minor child or, in certain states, an incapacitated person.

Incapacity—The inability to act on your own behalf as determined by applicable law.

Inter Vivos Trust—Any trust created during lifetime.

Intestacy, Intestate—A term that is applied when an individual dies without a will.

Irrevocable—Indicates something that cannot be changed or terminated.

Joint Tenancy with Right of Survivorship—A form of title that can be placed on property that is co-owned. At the death of one of the co-owners, the other will become the sole owner of the property by operation of law, regardless of what may be provided by the will.

Living Trust—A revocable trust established by a grantor during his or her lifetime.

Marital Deduction—A deduction allowing for the unlimited transfer of any or all property from one spouse to the other generally free of estate and gift tax.

Minor Child—A person who has not yet reached the legal age of majority. This age can differ from state to state, but generally is between 18 and 21.

Power of Attorney—A written legal document that gives an individual the authority to act for another.

Present Interest—A right to the immediate use, possession, and enjoyment of contributed property.

Probate—The process of proving a will before a court of law to ensure that it is authentic.

State Death or Inheritance Taxes—The tax imposed by the state in which you live and/or where your property is located, if different, on the transfer of that property to another at your death.

Testamentary Trust—A trust that is created upon your death by the terms of your will.

Trust Agreement—A written legal instrument created by a grantor during his or her lifetime or at death that sets the terms upon which a trustee or trustees will hold and manage property for the benefit of one or more beneficiaries.

Trustee—A person who holds legal title to assets and has a fiduciary obligation to manage those assets for the benefit of the beneficial owner of those assets.

Will—A legal document directing the administration and disposition of your property after your death.

THE LIVING WILL REGISTRY

If your family is unaware of your Advance Directive, or is unable to locate it, it is useless. To help solve that problem, many hospitals and healthcare facilities have relations with the U.S. Living Will Registry. The registry provides medical personnel and patients' families with Advance Directives whenever and wherever they are needed—if they have been filed with the registry.

You can mail your Advance Directive and Registration Agreement to the U.S. Living Will Registry, P.O. Box 2789, Westfield, NJ 07091-2789.

Additional information regarding the Living Will Registry can be obtained on the Internet at www.uslivingwillregistry.com.

By registering your Advance Directive with the U.S. Living Will Registry your directive will be stored in the Registry's computer database. At your request, the registry will send a copy of your directive to the hospital, nursing home, hospice, or other care facility where you are located and it will be kept as part of your confidential medical record.

If your health care professional is associated with the Living Will Registry they can register your Advance Directive for you. If they are not, you can contact them the Registry directly and they will register you for a fee.

CHAPTER THREE

THE FUNERAL

It is impossible that anything so natural, so necessary, and so universal as death, should ever have been designed by Providence as an evil to mankind.

—JONATHAN SWIFT (1667–1745)

Richmond Virginia's Hollywood Cemetery is situated on a scenic bluff overlooking the James River. It is the final resting place of three Presidents: James Monroe, John Tyler, and Confederate President Jefferson Davis. One of the first things visitors notice is the prevalence of family plots. It is the rare old Richmond family that does not have several generations buried in the same plot. The other thing you notice is that many of the people buried at Hollywood did not die in Richmond. President James Monroe died in New York City, and Jefferson Davis died in New Orleans. Of the 18,000 Civil War dead buried here, most fought and died far away, many at Gettysburg.

Spending a little time now thinking about and planning what type of funeral and burial you would like will make it much easier on your family. In addition, gathering all the vital information in one place that your survivors will need will be extremely helpful.

PARDON ME, IS THIS THE FAMILY PLOT?

So where do you want to be buried? In a family plot surrounded by your parents and grandparents or the last place you and your spouse lived? Do you want a ground burial, a mausoleum, a lawn crypt, or do you want to be cremated? Have you discussed your wishes with your family?

Before proceeding, let's explain and define a few terms:

- Ground burial remains the customary method of burial in the United States. A "plot" can vary in size from an individual space to a family "estate" in which room is reserved for future generations and set apart from other plots. Most cemeteries require a burial vault to protect the casket and prevent the ground from sinking.
- Mausoleums are stone or concrete crypts designed to hold the remains of the deceased. Some of the best-known monuments in history are mausoleums, including Egypt's pyramids and India's Taj Mahal. Private mausoleums offer prestige and personalization, as they can signify your family has been an important part of the community.
- Lawn crypts are actually small mausoleums designed primarily for two people who wish to be buried below rather than above ground.
- Cremated remains are usually deposited in an urn that can be placed in the home, a mausoleum, wall-niche, or buried in a family burial space. In some cases, the ashes are scattered in an area that has a special meaning to the deceased. Keep in mind that many localities require special permission to do this.

The first decision that your family needs to make after your death is about the funeral. This is a time of severe emotional turmoil for everyone involved and, unless you have done some preplanning, they will be asked to make a long list of decisions. Unfortunately, this is often *not* the time when everyone is thinking rationally. As a result the funeral home may talk your family into buying a "State Funeral" when all you wanted was a simple graveside service.

This is also the point at which individual family members can begin squabbling over funeral details and costs unless you have left instructions for them to follow.

You can do your loved ones a great favor by making arrangements while you are still well, able to make decisions, and can even do some comparison shopping. Preplanned funerals and cemetery plots are one of the kindest gifts that you can give to your loved ones. And they can save some money.

You should also look into what it takes to transport your remains if you wish to be taken from the place you die to another place for burial. Transportation can be a problem. Some years ago, a friend was taking his mother's ashes across the country for burial. Seeing the ashes, airport security wanted to run some tests to make sure he was not transporting illegal drugs. Only a certificate from the funeral director saved the day.

Funeral directors will make arrangements for transportation. Your family will need to supply information to the receiving funeral home as well as the home doing the shipping.

If you are a military veteran, the military has an office on virtually every base that will assist a survivor with the paperwork to arrange for a military burial or military ceremony at your funeral. To help your family, contact your nearest military facility for more information.

Visit your local funeral home to gather more information. Service Corporation, the nation's largest funeral provider, has a useful website at www.dignitymemorial.com. This will connect you to a network of funeral and cremation services and provide some helpful advice on the many choices you have.

Funerals and funeral homes are regulated by the Federal Trade Commission. There is even a rule, enforced by the FTC, called the "Funeral Rule." It is designed to prevent an unscrupulous funeral director from taking advantage of grieving relatives. The FTC has a useful website that tells you all about this and much more at www. ftc.gov/bcp/rulemaking/funeral/index.shtm.

The Funeral Rule requires funeral homes to provide you with a detailed list of their services and the prices for these services. Whether you have prepaid or just preplanned your funeral, make sure your family knows your wishes.

Before we begin to plan the funeral, let's get some essential facts down on paper. You are the only one who truly knows your personal history. On death, accurate personal information is required for legal paperwork to be issued. Beyond the legal forms, information is required for obituaries that will be published, and friends and relatives will need to be contacted. To save time and effort, it's a good idea to have all that information written down in one place.

NOTE TO THE FAMILY: THE FIRST THING TO DO WHEN SOMEONE DIES

When someone dies, the first thing to do is to notify the appropriate authorities. Most deaths occur in a hospital where staff and doctors know what to do about pronouncing death. The hospital staff will assist the family in contacting the funeral home.

If the death occurs at home, *dial 911* and an emergency response team will be dispatched to assist you. When the paramedics arrive, they will confirm death has occurred and usually will be able to determine the cause of death. Once death has been established, the funeral home can be contacted. If the family is a member of or attends a religious institution, the minister, priest or rabbi can also be called to provide grief counseling and help with funeral arrangements.

If death occurs while on travel, call 911, followed by a call to a funeral home in that area. They will prepare the body for shipment home and arrange for your local funeral home to receive the body.

PERSONAL INFORMATION NEEDED FOR THE FUNERAL PROCESS

Ever since Pharaohs ruled Egypt, births, marriages, and deaths have been subjects of record keeping. When a death occurs today, a surprising amount of information is recorded. The Personal Information section in the workbook is devoted to summarizing most of the information that is typically requested. Please take time now to fill it out.

FUNERAL DEALINGS
AND INTERNMENT DECISIONS

Once all the vital personal information has been listed and family and close friends have been notified, the next step is making what the funeral industry refers to as the "final arrangements."

You will, in all likelihood, want to have a local funeral home take care of them. If you and your family have dealt with a funeral director for many years, you can ask him or her to meet with you at your home or office to discuss the services they provide and what they cost.

In 2012, the average funeral service cost between $7,000 and $12,000. Minimal funerals involving either immediate burial or direct cremation can cost as little as $2,000.

With a more typical funeral, the family gets the following:

- Preparation (or cremation)
- Casket
- Vault
- Viewing
- Service
- Hearse
- Limousine for the family

In addition to these obvious items, the funeral home should also submit an obituary to the newspapers and send death notices to friends and relatives.

The Federal Trade Commission via the Funeral Rule requires that each funeral home provide you with a general price list that discloses the prices and services provided by the funeral home.

Once you have chosen the funeral home you wish to use, you can be sure that the details of your final arrangements will be handled with a minimum of trauma on the part of your loved ones. They will have the comfort of knowing that they are honoring your wishes.

With few exceptions, planning for death is not something anyone looks forward to. Keep in mind, however, that it's easier for someone to preplan the funeral arrangements while still alive than for the family to make the arrangements during a period of profound grief. A meeting with a funeral director should take no more than one to two hours, will provide you with all of the information you need, and will take a large burden from your family.

Cremation is gaining popularity among some segments of the population. Certain religions, however, are opposed to it. It can also be a contentious issue between members of a family. If your preference is cremation, make sure that your wishes are clearly stated. It would also be useful to discuss the issue with members of your family as well as a member of the clergy if you belong to a religious organization.

If you decide to be cremated, most of the other decisions regarding the funeral and religious services remain the same, with these obvious exceptions:

- There will be no viewing.
- There will be no casket; however, the urn can be on display.

Storage or disposal of the ashes includes everything from scattering them (be sure to have a permit), storing them at home, burying them, or placing them in a crypt.

If your family members plan to transport your ashes on an aircraft, it is important that they have a certificate from the funeral director or they risk problems with airport security.

Many local newspapers have pages devoted to death notices. You may wish to write your own, mentioning things for which you would like to be remembered. If you do, you may wish to use the section in the workbook devoted for that purpose.

RELIGIOUS SERVICES

If you belong to a church or synagogue, the clergy can be of tremendous aid to the family before, during, and after the funeral. The clergy members' most influential work is done in moments of crisis. They can be very helpful with grief counseling of the bereaved. In addition, they work closely with funeral directors. One of the advantages of being affiliated with a church or synagogue is that members of a congregation are usually available to help the family by providing food or even cleaning a home during the traumatic days after a death.

Religious services may be held in the funeral home, in a house of worship, or at the graveside. The location is partly determined by the customs of the denomination and even by the age of the deceased. Church funerals were most common 40 years ago, but the trend now is toward services in the funeral chapel. Graveside services are usually very small gatherings of family or very close friends.

Memorial service preplanning is important. You have the opportunity to specify the where and how of your own memorial service. If cost is important to you, be sure to ask the funeral director about the cost difference between having a service in the funeral chapel or in a house of worship.

The exact day and time of a service is at the request of the family, but is usually arranged between a funeral director and the clergyperson.

If you would like to preplan parts of your funeral service, your clergy will be happy to place your requests in the files at your house of worship.

If you have any special requests for ways to memorialize your passing, please note them in the workbook or on the information you give your clergy. Most clergy will be happy to accommodate any special requests, as long as they are notified well before the service. Surprising the minister, priest, or rabbi is never a good idea.

CHAPTER FOUR

FINANCIAL ACCOUNTING

Animals have these advantages over man: they never hear the clock strike, they die without any idea of death, they have no theologians to instruct them, their last moments are not disturbed by unwelcome and unpleasant ceremonies, their funerals cost them nothing, and no one starts lawsuits over their wills.

VOLTAIRE (1694-1778)

A few years ago I was reviewing a new client's estate planning documents when he showed me his trust agreement. It was comprehensive, detailed, and professional. There was only one problem with it: it was totally useless. A lot of the client's assets were held in a "joint tenants with rights of survivorship" (JTWROS) account and the rest of his assets were held in retirement accounts. No matter what his trust document said, at his death the jointly owned assets would go to his spouse and the assets in his retirement account would go to the named beneficiary, also his spouse. The client was shocked to learn that the trust agreement that cost him thousands of dollars in legal fees would not affect the distribution of his assets one iota. Who owns what—otherwise known as the titling of assets—overrides other considerations and often determines what happens at death.

Titling may be even more critical if a spouse becomes incapacitated. Mark (not his real name) kept all the family assets in his name

23

after marriage. This was not a major problem until he had an accident that left him totally incapacitated. His wife had to apply to the court to manage her husband's assets and had to account to the court for the way she managed his assets. This created severe problems for her as she had to record and justify every dollar she spent as well as posting a bond.

Because estate law is complex and the cost of making an erroneous decision regarding the division of assets can be great, it is highly recommended that an attorney specializing in estate planning be retained prior to death. Having a professional review all your estate documents and plans can prevent unforeseen issues such as those that Mark's wife had to deal with.

Your Will and Division of the Assets

Once the first few days of grieving are over, it is time for your survivors to address the issue of who receives your estate. If you are married and your spouse survives you, in most cases (but not all) the primary beneficiary is the surviving spouse.

Wills (and trusts—we'll get to those later) are very important. They are legal documents that direct your executor on how you wish for your assets to be divided. There are several points to keep in mind about the transfer of property after death:

1. **The way that property is owned ("titled") and/or named beneficiaries take precedence over the directives of a will.** This simply means that if you have an account jointly owned by you and your spouse with right of survivorship, your spouse will receive these assets irrespective of the terms of a will.
2. **If you do not have a will (to die "intestate" in legal terms) the laws of the state in which you reside determine how your estate will be distributed.** This may not be in keeping with your wishes, *so have a proper will or trust prepared prior to your death,* even if you plan to be immortal.
3. **Even if you have a will, it cannot override the laws of the state in terms of beneficiary designations.**

Many wealthy people, not willing to face their own mortality, have cost their heirs literally millions of dollars by failing to have a simple will drawn. It is important, even if your estate is not large, that you have a will properly drawn so that there is no question about your bequests. While large estates often enter the headlines as squabbling heirs hire platoons of lawyers to haggle over how many millions each one will get, anyone who has ever been involved in dividing small inheritances will testify that issues involving a few dollars often end in feuds that rival the Hatfields and the McCoys. More families have been split over who gets Grandma's silver spoons or Dad's gold watch than any other issue.

One of the most important considerations in drawing up your will is the choice of executor. An executor is the person named in your will to manage your estate. This person will collect your property, pay any debts and taxes, and distribute your property or assets according to your will. Executors should be reimbursed for their expenses and are often paid a fee for their services. Be sure that the person you choose to be your executor is willing and able to take on this responsibility.

Estate and tax law are constantly changing. So is the composition of your family and your personal wealth. It is important to have your will and/or trust documents reviewed every few years—or when you have a change in circumstances, such as a marriage or the death of an heir—to make sure they are up to date and meet your current needs and wishes.

You should keep a copy of your will in a secure place and have your attorney keep a copy in his or her files.

Where is your will? In the workbook, can you specify its location.

If for some reason you cannot deal with an attorney, there are websites available that will aid you in drafting a simple will. Doing a simple Internet search will give you many of options. They include, but are not limited to, the following:

http://www.legalzoom.com/legalzip/wills/will_procedure.html
http://www.legacywriter.com/
http://www.nolo.com/index.cfm

To better allow you to understand some of the more technical is-sues involving estates, what follows is a brief description of some of the issues that you may be required to address at death. It is not a complete review of the topics covered and does not address the legal or tax consequences associated with the topics discussed, nor is it an endorsement or recommendation on my part of the particular strategies discussed. This information is believed to be current as of this printing, but proper legal advice is always recommended since changes are frequent.

ESTATE TAX

The estate tax is a tax imposed on an estate at death. The amount of the tax depends on who inherits and the size of the estate at death.

PROPERTY TRANSFERRED AT DEATH

Assets owned by a decedent can be passed on to beneficiaries in a number of ways. For example, life insurance passes to beneficiaries that are named in the policy. Other assets that are transferred by ben-eficiary designation include annuities, IRAs, employee retirement plans, and payable-on-death and transfer-on-death accounts.

Assets held as joint tenants with right of survivorship will pass to the surviving joint tenant or tenants immediately upon the death of a joint tenant. These assets are not subject to probate and are not subject to the terms of a will.

Other assets you own when you die will be controlled by your will or, if you do not have a will, by the law of the state in which you reside at the time of your death.

Property in trust is discussed later.

ALLOWABLE DEDUCTIONS AND CREDITS

Currently, you may pass an unlimited amount of assets to your legal spouse, if he or she is a U.S. citizen. If your assets are passed to your spouse, they become part of her or his estate. Because estates above a certain level can be subject to high estate taxes at death, it may ben-efit you to consult with an attorney to determine if there are ways of minimizing the estate tax on the death of the second-to-die.

Keep in mind that the way property is titled often determines who receives the assets at death without regard for wills or trusts.

JOINTLY HELD PROPERTY

If spouses hold property jointly, one-half of the value of the property will be included in the estate of the spouse who is the first to die. All of the property will automatically pass to the surviving spouse estate-tax free due to the marital deduction. Generally, the surviving spouse will receive a step-up in tax cost basis to fair market value for only one-half of the property.

In some cases, property is owned jointly with someone who is not a spouse. Consult an attorney to determine how this affects any taxes owed.

Property may also be titled as "tenants in common." Property owned in this manner will pass under the terms of the decedent's will and not by operation of law.

Some states also have some form of a community property system to determine the interest of husband and wife in property acquired during marriage. Generally, under a community property system, all property acquired during marriage is deemed owned one-half by each spouse, regardless of the titling of the property. Consult your attorney to see if this applies to you and what this means at death.

THE BASICS OF LIFETIME GIFT GIVING

Any person can give $13,000 (the "annual exclusion" as of 2012) each year to any number of donees without either incurring a gift-tax liability or affecting the estate-tax exemption. This can change at the will of Congress. Gifting is often used to reduce the taxable estate for high net worth individuals or families.

USING YOUR LIFETIME GIFT-TAX EXEMPTION

In addition to making gifts using the annual exclusion, you may wish to consider making gifts in an amount equal to your lifetime exemption. If your wealth is significant enough that you can afford to gift your lifetime exemption now, you can reduce your current taxable estate and remove the future growth from your estate. Once your lifetime exemption is exhausted, future gifts over and above the annual exclusion will be subject to gift tax. You should discuss the appropriateness of making taxable gifts that result in the payment of gift tax with your tax and legal advisor. Making lifetime gifts without incurring gift tax provides several benefits: the gifted asset is removed from your estate, and the post-gift appreciation of the property is generally removed from your estate.

TRUSTS

Trusts are used for a variety of purposes. Trusts can be created and funded during your lifetime, or they can be created by the terms of a will.

Trusts involve a grantor, a trustee, and one or more beneficiaries. A trust is often used as a substitute for a will. A grantor changes the ownership of assets, such as investments, to the trust and either names himself as trustee, has others act as joint trustees, or names an institution as trustee. A trust names the beneficiaries of the assets in the trust, who then receive the assets in the trust at the grantor's death. The terms of a trust may allow it to be changed or even revoked by the grantor, or the trust terms may be fixed or irrevocable at the date of creation. This flexibility allows the grantor to use a trust to meet his or her specific personal objectives.

Here are the three primary reasons trusts are used:

- Reduce estate taxes
- Avoid probate
- Take care of special needs beneficiaries

Trust documents have become increasingly popular as a means of passing assets from one person to another. One of the benefits of trusts is that they bypass the process known as "probate." They are especially important if your assets are large enough to incur estate taxes ("death taxes"). You are allowed to pass an unlimited amount of assets to your spouse free of an estate tax. Eventually the spouse will also die. It's at this point that an estate tax may be due for non-spousal heirs. For people of even moderate wealth, estate taxes may be due when non-spousal heirs are beneficiaries. Trusts are often used to increase the amount that you may leave to your children—free of estate tax—on the death of your spouse, often referred to as the "second death."

A federal estate tax is levied on estates in excess of a certain amount that is not left to a spouse. As of 2012, the estate tax exclusion (the amount that can be passed without tax) is found in the following table. Please be aware that Congress is constantly tinkering with the provisions of the federal estate tax. Also, since the federal government has raised the amount that can be passed on to heirs not subject to the federal estate tax, the individual states are in the process of changing their own estate tax laws.

Year	Estate Tax "Exclusion"	Maximum Tax Rate
2001	$ 675,000	55%
2002	$1,000,000	50%
2003	$1,000,000	49%
2004	$1,500,000	48%
2005	$1,500,000	47%
2006	$2,000,000	46%
2007	$2,000,000	45%
2008	$2,000,000	45%
2009	$3,500,000	45%
2010	Tax repeal	0%
2011	$5,000,000	35%
2012	$5,000,000	35%

Note that after 2012, by current law, the estate tax reverts to the rates that were in effect in 2002. Congress is expected to address this issue.

In any case, I strongly recommend that you review your situation with a specialist in estate planning so that the proper documents can be prepared, the assets properly titled, and the beneficiaries properly named on your retirement accounts, annuities, and life insurance policies. This is not the time for do-it-yourself estate planning. Saving a few dollars on attorney fees now can potentially cost your heirs thousands later.

The reason that trusts are almost, but not quite, a substitute for wills is that there are certain assets that are usually not put into a trust. These include most tangible personal property, such as automobiles, collections, antiques, and Grandma's silver spoons. As I mentioned earlier, don't take a chance on causing a family rift by overlooking these items. If they are worthwhile or are likely to have emotional or financial value, mention them and specify who is to get these items. If you can't decide, you may want to tell your family to hold an estate sale and divide the proceeds. The benefit of a sale is that it allows the heirs who really want some of these items to bid and buy them.

There are various types of trusts. Some examples:

Bypass Trust—Bypass trusts are used to preserve the lifetime estate tax exemption that everyone has prior to death. If the first spouse to die passes all his assets to his spouse, that exemption is lost. For that reason, trusts can be set up that pass a certain amount of property to what is usually referred to as a bypass trust. The surviving spouse may be allowed to receive all the income from this trust or give the trustee discretion to invade the principal for the benefit of the spouse.

Qualified Terminable Interest Property Trust (QTIP)—A QTIP Trust is often used to provide for a spouse during her lifetime but to have the assets pass to the decedent's children on the spouse's death. It is often used in the case of a second marriage.

Irrevocable Life Insurance Trusts (ILITs)—An ILIT can be used to provide cash to pay estate taxes and to pass along assets to heirs outside of the taxable estate. An ILIT is often set up to own a life insurance policy which pays beneficiaries on the death of a second spouse. There are specific rules regarding the ownership of an ILIT and the manner in which insurance premiums are paid. Setting up an ILIT requires the services of a good estate planning attorney to avoid the proceeds of the insurance policy being drawn back into the estate.

Generation-Skipping Trust (GST)—A type of trust in which the grantor leaves assets to grandchildren instead of children. The purpose of a GST is to reduce estate taxes. For example, if an estate is large enough and is left to the children it can be taxed up to the maximum tax rate. When the children die and leave it to their children, there would be another estate tax. With a GST, one of these taxes is eliminated. There is a limitation on the amount that can be placed in a GST free of taxes and that amount has been changed frequently, so you should consult your attorney and financial advisor regarding this issue. Generation-skipping trusts can still be used to provide some financial benefits to a grantor's children because any income generated by the trust's assets can be made accessible to the grantor's children while still leaving the assets in trust for his or her grandchildren.

Be sure to record the location of your trust documents, the name and contact information of the attorney who prepared them, and any special instructions about them. You may use the workbook to do so.

LIFE INSURANCE

Are you worth more dead than alive? According to published reports, more than 25 percent of all life insurance policy benefits go unpaid after death. Insurers make virtually no effort to find lost beneficiaries and heirs. That is not their job. To make sure your beneficiaries receive the benefits of your insurance policies, you need to keep your records current.

You should review your life insurance policies annually. The life insurance industry, like all industries, is constantly evolving, bringing out new products, and tweaking old ones. Over the last few decades, insurance companies have adopted new actuarial tables reflecting the fact that people are living longer. The net effect of this is that newer insurance policies are often less expensive than older policies. Another way of looking at this is that you may be able to shop around and get more life insurance for the same amount of money.

Most people have one or more life insurance policies. If you have several policies, it is important for your beneficiaries to be aware of them and know how to contact the insurance company(s).

You should gather all of your policies in a single place and make a list of the policies that are in force. If you have misplaced any policies, ask your agent for a copy of the contract.

What do you want your family to do with the proceeds of your life insurance policies? Life insurance proceeds are free of income taxes, but not necessarily estate taxes. You should get the advice of a competent estate planning attorney to make sure that your family, not the tax man, receives most of the benefits of the policy.

In some cases, life insurance proceeds are substantial and can make a significant difference in how survivors live. The life insurance section of the workbook gives you a place to record advice for your survivors about how your life insurance proceeds should be managed.

SAFE DEPOSIT BOXES

My wife and I have had a safe deposit box for many years with a local bank. Mega Bank swallowed up Local Bank last year, and we got a notice that our box had been moved. Luckily the new location is only a few blocks from the old one. But it made us think about the purpose of this box, and we decided to inspect its contents.

Keep a list of the items in your safe deposit box. Having such a list will, at minimum, save you a trip to the box in vain if you forget where you put a certain document and mistakenly believe it's in the safe deposit box.

If you use a safe deposit box at a local bank, your family may be required to get into it after your death.

Keep in mind that banks restrict access to safe deposit boxes to those people who have signed a signature card. If you die and your name is the only one authorized to access the safe deposit box, your family could have trouble gaining access to your box.

For this reason, make sure that your box allows your spouse or trusted relative to have access to it, or avoid storing anything in a safe deposit box that requires immediate access on your death. It's best to give one of the two keys the bank gives you to the person who is on your signature card with you.

I will use this opportunity to get on my soapbox and urge everyone: **DO NOT STORE STOCKS, BONDS, OR OTHER FINANCIAL INSTRUMENTS IN A SAFE DEPOSIT BOX. PUT THEM IN A BROKERAGE ACCOUNT.**

Perhaps as a residue of the Great Depression, some people still insist on holding on to paper stock and bond certificates and storing them in a safe deposit box. It may make you feel safer, but it creates a nightmare for your family. Transferring ownership of paper certificates is both costly and time consuming. Worse, if certificates get lost in the mail, the replacement cost can vary from hundreds to thousands of dollars. Don't put your spouse or children through this or force them to hire an attorney (who starts the money clock running when you call him) to do it for them. Holding paper certificates makes as much sense as keeping your family fortune in dollar bills. Don't do it.

INVESTMENT ACCOUNTS

In 1945, two brothers, Jacob and Samuel, were rescued from the Nazi extermination camp of Buchenwald. The rest of their family had been killed. The brothers joined other refugees that left Europe after World War II. Jacob came to the United States, became an engineer, and worked many years for a major corporation. Samuel immigrated to Australia and became an accountant.

Several years ago, Jacob died. He had never married. Samuel—by now quite elderly—came to the United States to settle Jacob's affairs. What he found was financial chaos. Jacob had always lived frugally and invested widely. Unfortunately, he kept very poor records. Samuel spent several weeks rummaging through files, boxes, drawers, and even under couch pillows trying to gather together all the certificates, statements, and even uncashed dividend checks that Jacob had left behind. We will never be certain that all of Jacob's assets have been located.

Few people leave behind as chaotic a financial tangle as Jacob did, but I find that more than half of the people I advise after a death are not certain that they can identify all of a deceased's investment assets.

The first lesson from this example is this: **DO NOT KEEP STOCK OR BOND CERTIFICATES AT HOME OR IN A SAFE DEPOSIT BOX. KEEP ALL FINANCIAL ASSETS IN BROKERAGE ACCOUNTS.**

Modern brokerage accounts now allow access via checkbook, electronic funds transfer (EFT) and charge cards. Have all dividends and interest payments deposited in your account; and, if you need cash, you may write a check. There is no reason for your heirs to search through your papers to find uncashed dividend checks.

As people get older, financial advisors and estate planning attorneys often advise clients to consolidate their assets. This is sound advice and greatly simplifies the job of managing an estate at death. It is often possible to consolidate assets—even mutual funds that you have bought outside of a brokerage account—with a single financial advisor or team of advisors. This has the advantage of giving your financial advisor a better view of your assets and thus providing more comprehensive plans and advice. It also makes it easier for the surviving spouse or heirs to identify your investment assets.

Investment accounts with brokerage firms, money managers, and mutual funds typically make up the bulk of the assets of most families. It is not unusual for a family to have multiple accounts.

Be sure to make a list of your investment accounts. You may use the investment section of the workbook to do so.

Corporate Benefit Plans and Assets

Corporations offer benefit plans that may have assets in them at your death. These include 401(k) plans—or similar plans such as 403(b) plans, 457 plans, TSP plans—deferred compensation plans, or stock option plans. These become the property of the designated beneficiary at your death. It is important to review your beneficiary designation regularly and after any major life events (death, divorce, etc.) to make sure the person named is still the person you wish to receive these assets, however, your beneficiary has to know they exist.

One of the biggest mistakes people make when they change employers it to leave the 401(k) (or similar) account behind. When switching employers, take the opportunity to roll the assets into an individual retirement account (IRA) so that you can take advantage of the incredible variety of investment options that are available to you and to ensure that the account does not become an "orphan" that your heirs do not know exists.

It has been my experience that investment assets held in corporate plans in the name of a deceased person require an extraordinary amount of paperwork to have them transferred to a spouse or other beneficiary. It is generally easier to deal with your investment advisor who uses a reputable custodian and will help your spouse with the red tape. Consolidation of assets with a Registered Investment Advisor (RIA) makes life much easier for spouses and heirs. If some of your assets are held by corporate benefits departments, the staff will typically help your heirs in identifying these assets. You should let your family know what benefits you have and guide them on what to do with them after your death.

Take time now to record pertinent information in the workbook about your corporate benefit plans, deferred compensation, and stock options.

Other Investments

Other than your personal residence, investment real estate is frequently a source of both wealth and income. Be sure to list all other investments you have in the appropriate section in the workbook.

CHAPTER FIVE

Financial Management

Remembering that I'll be dead soon is the most important tool I've ever encountered to help me make the big choices in life.

Steve Jobs
Stanford Commencement Address, 2005

W hen Pam's (not her real name) husband died, leaving her with three children to raise on her own, she thought the insurance benefits would be more than enough to make her financially independent. She installed a pool and made other major improvements to the family home. Unfortunately, the money did not stretch as far or last as long as she imaged. Looking back she wishes she had invested more of the money and done some other things differently, including securing the help of a professional financial advisor earlier.

INVESTMENT MANAGEMENT

If you have been the one building and managing the family fortune over the years, one of the most difficult things for your survivor(s) is knowing how to manage the family assets after you are gone. Investing the family estate is not a job for amateurs. Even professionals are not right all of the time. I strongly recommend that you find a professional that you can trust who can advise your family on the appropriate asset allocation and investment vehicles that will allow your spouse and/or children or other heirs to enjoy the benefits of the assets you have built during your lifetime.

While no one would go to a dentist and ask that professional to perform brain surgery, many people go to their lawyer, accountant, or insurance agent for investment guidance. It is always a grave mistake to get advice from people who are not specialists in their field. For that reason, as a financial advisor, I refer my clients to their accountants for tax guidance and to their lawyers for legal advice. As a professional, I know my areas of expertise and they know theirs. When guiding your heirs, it is important that you let them know these basic truths.

Keep a few points in mind when advising your beneficiaries from the great beyond:

- First, things change, and plans that look bulletproof today may be bullet riddled tomorrow. Investing is a dynamic process, and no one can guarantee that today's strong company will not be tomorrow's bankruptcy. Examples abound: Penn Central, GM, Enron, WorldCom, Lucent, Polaroid, Kodak, and so forth. One of the primary methods of avoiding catastrophic losses is to diversify your assets. If a single stock or bond represents more than 10 percent of your assets, you may be taking too much risk.

- By far the most common reason given for an unwillingness to diversify is taxes. People are extremely reluctant to sell highly appreciated assets—even if they have grown to be way more than 10% of your total assets—because of the tax bill this triggers. *Death eliminates this problem.* On death, the "tax cost basis" of an asset gets adjusted to the value of the asset on the date of death. If assets are held jointly, it is assumed that half of the assets get this tax cost basis adjustment. The bottom line is this: on death, assets that have been held by the deceased because it cost too much in taxes to sell them can now be sold and the assets redeployed without triggering a big capital gains tax bill.

- Certificates of Deposits (CDs) were once considered the best way of keeping your money safe. While your principal was government guaranteed, the interest they paid dropped steadily, going from 15 percent in 1978 to 1 percent (or less) in 2012. As a result, those who depended on their CD interest payments for income were devastated. Government guarantees against loss do not guarantee you the income you need to live.

- When you are gone, your spouse—if he or she survives you—will have different objectives than when you were alive. His or her income from guaranteed sources, such as pension payments and Social Security, may go down. As a result, it is possible that the investments may have to be altered to generate more income. This should be discussed with your spouse as well as your family's financial advisor

If you use an advisor, get to know him or her personally. After all, the well-being of your family may depend on his or her advice. You don't want to take advice from a stranger. Personal chemistry is as important as professional experience and credibility. Can you get along with this advisor?

The person you want advising you and your family should take a holistic approach. You don't want someone that tries to sell you the "hot stock" as your family advisor. You want someone who will understand you and your family's needs and devise a plan that will achieve your objectives with the lowest possible risk.

Determine the length of time your prospective advisor has been in the investment business. Who is their typical client? Does he or she have any advanced training? Are they a CERTIFIED FINANCIAL PLANNER™ professional? Does he or she limit the number of clients they work with so that your family will get the service that they deserve? Is he or she part of a team, and are there assistants? What will happen if he or she retires or dies?

Finding someone who can help your family once you are gone will be a great gift to those you leave behind.

TYPES OF ASSETS MANAGEMENT

You and your survivors have choices about the type of asset management you use. Some people choose to manage their assets themselves. Others choose an outside professional wealth management specialist or an independent Registered Investment Advisor.

SELF-MANAGED ACCOUNTS

There are several reasons why people wish to self-manage portfolios: fear of losing control, sentimental attachment to certain assets, discomfort with an outside manager, concern with capital gains and losses, or the costs associated with hiring an outside manager.

Unless the person managing the assets is experienced, this approach is usually penny-wise but pound-foolish. The amateur investor is typically at a disadvantage compared to the professional in terms of access to timely information and the ability to process the information that is available. Information today is free and virtually everywhere. Knowing what to do with it is both an art and a science.

Another advantage of using seasoned investment advisors is that professionals are less likely to allow emotions to cloud their judgment regarding investments. The advent of 24-hour, 7-days-a-week financial programs on TV and the availability of Internet solicitations often leads the average investor to react emotionally to events that are not in his or her best interest.

Your financial advisor should be able to show you that he or she has a planned, disciplined investment strategy and should be able to explain it in fairly simple terms.

More and more, financial advisors advise their clients to use outside managers to manage client assets whenever possible (see "Managed Accounts").

Large institutions do not manage their own assets; they hire outside experts. It makes sense for individuals to do the same.

MANAGED ACCOUNTS

Managed accounts are accounts consisting of individual securities that are managed on a discretionary basis by an outside manager.

These accounts are usually "wrapped." That means that they are managed for an all-inclusive fee that includes the management fee and transaction costs. In other words, there are no separate commissions for buying or selling securities.

Most brokerage firms have programs like this available. Typically, the minimum account size is $100,000 and the fee is calculated as a percentage of the assets in the account. Keep in mind that individual managers are like mutual funds in one respect: they are style specific. That means that a manager may focus on investing only in U.S. government bonds or stocks in small foreign companies. Therefore, to be properly diversified among different asset classes, it may be necessary to hire multiple managers. A corollary of this is that doing so takes quite a sizeable pool of money. For family assets over $1 million dollars, this approach may be considered.

Individually managed accounts may have certain advantages over mutual funds. Those advantages include the following:

- No embedded capital gains (or losses)
- Customization—you can exclude certain stocks or industries
- Transparency—unlike mutual funds, you know exactly what you own

MUTUAL FUNDS

One of the most common ways people invest their money is through mutual funds. Mutual funds are pools of assets—stocks, bonds, or other financial assets—managed by professional managers, who use these pooled assets to invest in securities. They are managed by professional money managers in a manner consistent with the fund's objective.

The kinds of investments the mutual funds make are defined by the document known as the "prospectus." A fund's prospectus defines the kind of securities that a fund can own, the fees that the investor pays in return for professional management, and anything else that the manager needs to disclose in order to pass muster by the Securities and Exchange Commission (SEC).

Mutual funds are popular because they allow investors with a modest amount of money (sometimes as little as $25) to get professional help with their investments as well as a diversified portfolio of stocks and/or bonds.

While mutual funds are popular ways of investing money, the choices available can be confusing. There are more mutual funds available than there are stocks on the New York Stock Exchange. They offer investors a bewildering array of investment choices: everything from an investment in a broad index like the Standard & Poor's 500 to funds that invest only in Russian stocks. The selection of mutual funds must be considered within an overall strategy that takes into consideration the amount of risk that you are willing to accept, your time horizon, and your investment objectives.

Mutual funds, like any investment vehicle, should be viewed as long-term investments.

Mutual funds are not government guaranteed and are subject to market risk.

ASSET ALLOCATION PROGRAMS

Advisors realize that today's hot stock, industry, or economy can be tomorrow's train wreck. The way to reduce the risk of getting your family assets depleted as a result of overexposure to any one company, industry, or country is to diversify. The question is: what is the proper diversification for you and your family?

The investment industry is becoming increasingly sophisticated regarding the planning process and finding ways of diversifying away risk.

At our firm we begin by identifying the client's goals, time horizon, and risk tolerance. This then leads to an investment plan that strives to meet the objectives within the comfort level of the client.

The end result is usually an asset allocation decision that may include some or all of the following investment categories:

- Large Cap value stocks
- Large Cap growth stocks
- Small/medium Cap value stocks

- Small/medium Cap growth stocks
- Emerging market stocks
- U.S. short/intermediate term taxable bonds
- U.S. long term taxable bonds
- U.S. tax free bonds (municipals)
- Large Cap foreign stocks
- Foreign bonds
- Cash
- Commodities
- Precious metals
- Futures
- Currencies

This is by no means a complete or exhaustive list of investment categories. It is merely a brief list of some of the most popular asset classes that are available to the public today.

Asset Allocation Programs are designed to put together a financial portfolio consisting of some or all of these asset classes to achieve the family's financial goals. The proper mix is based on an evaluation of many factors including an individual's risk tolerance, return objectives, time horizon, and need for income.

CHAPTER SIX

BALANCING INCOME AND EXPENSES

Even though work stops, expenses run on.

CATO THE ELDER
On Agriculture, (234 BC–149 BC)

I have been the facilitator of Dave Ramsey's "Financial Peace University" several times. It's an excellent course designed to give people a basic understanding of financial principles. Most of the people who take the course are trying to work their way out of debt and learn how to save and invest. The biggest thing I learned by teaching the course was how little people know about budgeting and what it actually costs to run a household. People go into debt, owing thousands of dollars to credit card companies and paying astronomical interest rates because they don't keep track of what they spend and match their spending to their income. So it's no surprise that when a loved one passes on, the survivor often doesn't know what it costs to pay the household expenses.

Part of your legacy will be what income and expenses you leave behind.

INCOME SOURCES

Remember Sue from the introduction? She did not know what her income was or where it was coming from. Lacking this information, she did not know how much she could spend without dipping into her savings and investments. It is vital that your spouse knows how much income she or he has, and what the sources of income are.

Take time to record the sources of income your survivors may have in the worbook. Remember to include information about any pensions, investment portfolios, or income from rental units, as well as Social Security. Keep in mind that income that you receive, such as pension or Social Security payments, may not be the same for your spouse after your death.

SOCIAL SECURITY

When a Social Security recipient dies, the survivors need to contact the Social Security Administration at **1-800-772-1213**, between the hours of 7 A.M. and 7 P.M. on business days. Whenever you call, have your Social Security number handy. Please note that the following information may have changed by the time you read this, so always check with the Social Security Administration for current benefits.

Social Security survivor's benefits can be paid to qualified person(s):

- A widow/widower—full benefits at full retirement age (currently age 66 rising to age 67 if you were born in 1962 or later), or reduced benefits as early as age 60. (See http://www. socialsecurity.gov/survivorplan/survivorchartred.htm).
- A disabled widow/widower—as early as age 50.
- A widow/widower at any age if he or she takes care of the deceased's child who is under age 16 or disabled, and receiving Social Security benefits.
- Unmarried children under 18, or up to age 19 if they are attending high school full time. Under certain circumstances, benefits can be paid to stepchildren, grandchildren, or adopted children.

- Children at any age who were disabled before age 22 and remain disabled.
- Dependent parents age 62 or older.

The Social Security Administration has a website at www.socialsecurity.gov. The following information was copied from the Social Security website:

*When you apply for the Social Security death benefit, we will ask you:**

- *Your name and social security number;*
- *The deceased worker's name, gender, date of birth and social security number;*
- *The deceased worker's date and place of death;*
- *Whether the deceased worker ever filed for Social Security benefits, Medicare or Supplemental Security Income (if so, we will also ask for information on whose Social Security record he or she applied);*
- *Whether the deceased worker was unable to work because of illnesses, injuries or conditions at any time during the 14 months before his or her death (if "Yes," we will also ask when he or she became unable to work);*
- *Whether the deceased worker was ever in the active military service (if "Yes," we will also ask for the dates of his or her service);*
- *Whether the deceased worker worked for the railroad industry for 7 years or more;*
- *Whether the deceased worker earned social security credits under another country's social security system;*
- *The names, dates of birth (or age) and social security numbers (if known) of any of the deceased worker's former spouses and the dates of the marriages and how and when they ended;*
- *The names of any of the deceased worker's unmarried children under 18, 18–19 and in secondary school or disabled prior to age 22;*
- *The amount of the deceased worker's earnings in the year of death and the preceding year;*

---

* From the Social Security web site: www.ssa.gov

- *Whether the deceased worker had a parent who was dependent on the worker for 1/2 of his or her support at the time of the worker's death; and*
- *Whether the deceased worker and surviving spouse were living together at the time of death.*

If you are the surviving spouse, we will also ask:

- *Whether you have been unable to work because of illnesses, injuries or conditions at any time within the past 14 months (if "Yes," we will also ask when you became unable to work);*
- *Whether you or anyone else ever filed for Social Security benefits, Medicare or Supplemental Security Income on your behalf (if so, we will also ask for information on whose Social Security record you applied); and*
- *The names, dates of birth (or age) and social security numbers (if known) of any of your former spouses and the dates of the marriages and how and when they ended.*

If you are not the surviving spouse, we will also ask for the surviving spouse's name and address.

You also should bring along your checkbook or other papers that show your account number at a bank, credit union or other financial institution so you can sign up for Direct Deposit, [see http://www.socialsecurity.gov/deposit/] and avoid worries about lost or stolen checks and mail delays.

Social Security benefits for a surviving spouse, dependent minor children, or dependent parents are complex and should be discussed with the Social Security Administration. As a general rule, if both individuals in a couple are over retirement age and one dies, the surviving spouse is eligible for the higher of their benefit or the deceased spouse's benefit.

A final note: Your spouse or minor child may be eligible for a one-time $225 death benefit.

Contact the Social Security Administration for your particular benefits.

Expenses and Bills

Shortly after the funeral, the bills will begin to arrive. If you have been the one paying the bills, you should leave some instructions regarding bill paying. Surviving spouses are frequently unsure of the income they will need to maintain their lifestyle. Making a list of bills, how they are paid, and the amount, will be useful for budgeting and in creating a portfolio designed to meet their income needs. Turn to the workbook for a handy chart where you can list typical expenses.

The conventional way of paying bills is to write checks as bills come in. The advent of the Internet, however, has transformed bill paying into a much more automated process.

Some bills may be paid via automatic withdrawals from your checking account. On the other hand, you may be paying your bills electronically via an Internet bill-paying program with your bank, credit card, or brokerage firm.

If your spouse is not familiar with the process you are using, leave instructions on the method you use to pay bills.

If you pay bills electronically, your successor needs to know the web address for the bill-paying website, your user ID, and your password. Take time to record that information in the workbook. Be sure to review this information annually since you may change your password now and then. If you don't, you should think about doing so to protect against online fraud and identity theft.

Also be sure to list the bills that are paid via automatic withdrawals and the name of the account from which those bills are paid.

Other issues can also arise, such as cars or homes that are titled in the name of the deceased. The creditors are going to want to receive their payments and the ownership is going to have to be changed. It is important that this be done soon. The executor of an estate needs a court appointment to make the necessary changes, but these forms are usually good for only 60 days after which a new court appointment is needed.

On death, certain debts such as Federal student loans are forgiven; however, private debt becomes a claim against the estate. This is a

good reason to review life insurance policies to see if they are suffi-
cient to cover debts as well as maintenance of the survivor's lifestyle.
Banks offer mortgage insurance, but the premiums are often much
higher than a simple term policy that covers you during the time you
have a mortgage.

CHAPTER SEVEN

Annual Review

Cowards die many times before their deaths;
The valiant never taste of death but once.

—William Shakespeare

C ourage is facing difficult issues head on. Love is doing something for others without expecting anything in return.

This book guides you in preparing a gift you will leave to those you love. Having the courage to face your own mortality and putting your affairs in order now is a final testimony to your love. You wish to lighten grief, to remove some of the burden of parting, and to do an act of kindness and consideration for those you hold dear. Congratulations on your bravery.

Once you have completed the workbook, you have two jobs remaining: (1) make loved ones aware of the book's existence; and (2) review and update it annually.

Inform Others

Show the workbook or instructions you created, or at least talk about its existence, to your spouse, adult children, or other responsible people whom you expect to survive you. If you mention it in a calm, matter-of-fact way, then the conversation shouldn't become morbid or depressing. Keep your focus upbeat.

Remember you have gathered all your information in one place as a way to show how much you love your family. You might even give a copy of this book to your loved ones and encourage them to begin preparing their affairs as well. Be sure your spouse and children know where your workbook can be found. If you feel that it contains information you do not yet wish to share, then entrust the book to someone who can turn it over to your loved ones immediately upon your death.

The workbook portion should be kept in a secure location as it may contain information that is private, such as safe combinations, passwords, and PIN numbers. Take steps to make certain it does not become misplaced or get into the wrong hands.

Perform an Annual Review

Many employers perform an annual review of their employees' performance. If done properly, it can be a positive encounter that encourages workers and employers alike to continue striving toward shared goals. An annual review of the information you gathered in the workbook can provide similar encouragement for you to continue to strive to show your love for your family.

Consider setting a consistent date when you will perform your review of the information in the workbook. Perhaps you might review things on your birthday, on New Year's Day, when you set your clocks each spring and fall, or when you change your smoke detector batteries.

The date you choose does not matter. What matters is that you keep the information current. Your finances will evolve, and you will lose old friends and make new ones. You may move and have to review your funeral arrangements. Whatever you do, keep the information in the workbook current. And keep it in an easy-to-find place.

About the Author

ARIE J. KORVING is Chairman and co-founder of Korving & Company, LLC. Korving & Company provides financial advice and services to individuals, families, businesses, and nonprofit organizations. As people are living longer, retirees' concerns about outliving their financial assets has intensified. His firm specializes in helping people prepare for retirement, manage their finances during retirement, and plan their estate. With more than 50 years of combined experience, Mr. Korving and his team have found that their guidance is especially useful to those who become suddenly single through the death of a spouse or a divorce.

Prior to Korving & Company, Mr. Korving was First Vice President, Investments with UBS. He has held management positions with General Electric and earned a B.S. in Chemistry from Michigan Technological University. He has been a CERTIFIED FINANCIAL PLANNER™ practitioner since 1993.

He currently resides in Virginia with his wife of over 40 years. He has two children of which he's exceptionally proud, and a growing number of grandchildren.

In his spare time he is an avid reader, gardener, photographer, and traveler.